There is no need to forget your login details and passwords again! Simply write them down in this book to have them in easy reach when you need them.

There is room in the front of the book for your most-visited websites. Then you will find an A-Z listing with space for 16 websites for each letter. If you need extra space for any letter, use the spare pages at the back.

Make sure to keep the book safe and secure!

Website:
URL:
Username:
Password:
Notes:

Website:
URL:
Username:
Password:
Notes:

Website:
URL:
Username:
Password:
Notes:

Website:
URL:
Username:
Password:
Notes:

Website:

URL:

Username:

Password:

Notes:

---

Website:

URL:

Username:

Password:

Notes:

---

Website:

URL:

Username:

Password:

Notes:

---

Website:

URL:

Username:

Password:

Notes:

Website:

URL:

Username:

Password:

Notes:

Website:

URL:

Username:

Password:

Notes:

Website:

URL:

Username:

Password:

Notes:

Website:

URL:

Username:

Password:

Notes:

Website:

URL:

Username:

Password:

Notes:

Website:

URL:

Username:

Password:

Notes:

Website:

URL:

Username:

Password:

Notes:

Website:

URL:

Username:

Password:

Notes:

Website:
URL:
Username:
Password:
Notes:

---

Website:
URL:
Username:
Password:
Notes:

---

Website:
URL:
Username:
Password:
Notes:

---

Website:
URL:
Username:
Password:
Notes:

Website:
URL:
Username:
Password:
Notes:



Website:
URL:
Username:
Password:
Notes:



Website:
URL:
Username:
Password:
Notes:



Website:
URL:
Username:
Password:
Notes:

**A**

Website:
URL:
Username:
Password:
Notes:



Website:
URL:
Username:
Password:
Notes:



Website:
URL:
Username:
Password:
Notes:



Website:
URL:
Username:
Password:
Notes:

Website:
URL:
Username:
Password:
Notes:

Website:
URL:
Username:
Password:
Notes:

Website:
URL:
Username:
Password:
Notes:

Website:
URL:
Username:
Password:
Notes:

**A**

Website:
URL:
Username:
Password:
Notes:

Website:
URL:
Username:
Password:
Notes:

Website:
URL:
Username:
Password:
Notes:

Website:
URL:
Username:
Password:
Notes:

Website:
URL:
Username:
Password:
Notes:

Website:
URL:
Username:
Password:
Notes:

Website:
URL:
Username:
Password:
Notes:

Website:
URL:
Username:
Password:
Notes:

**B**

Website:
URL:
Username:
Password:
Notes:

Website:
URL:
Username:
Password:
Notes:

Website:
URL:
Username:
Password:
Notes:

Website:
URL:
Username:
Password:
Notes:

Website:

URL:

Username:

Password:

Notes:


Website:

URL:

Username:

Password:

Notes:


Website:

URL:

Username:

Password:

Notes:


Website:

URL:

Username:

Password:

Notes:

**B**

Website:
URL:
Username:
Password:
Notes:

Website:
URL:
Username:
Password:
Notes:

Website:
URL:
Username:
Password:
Notes:

Website:
URL:
Username:
Password:
Notes:

**B**

Website:
URL:
Username:
Password:
Notes:

Website:
URL:
Username:
Password:
Notes:

Website:
URL:
Username:
Password:
Notes:

Website:
URL:
Username:
Password:
Notes:

**C**

Website:
URL:
Username:
Password:
Notes:

Website:
URL:
Username:
Password:
Notes:

Website:
URL:
Username:
Password:
Notes:

Website:
URL:
Username:
Password:
Notes:

**C**

Website:
URL:
Username:
Password:
Notes:

Website:
URL:
Username:
Password:
Notes:

Website:
URL:
Username:
Password:
Notes:

Website:
URL:
Username:
Password:
Notes:

**C**

Website:
URL:
Username:
Password:
Notes:

Website:
URL:
Username:
Password:
Notes:

Website:
URL:
Username:
Password:
Notes:

Website:
URL:
Username:
Password:
Notes:

**C**

Website:
URL:
Username:
Password:
Notes:


Website:
URL:
Username:
Password:
Notes:


Website:
URL:
Username:
Password:
Notes:


Website:
URL:
Username:
Password:
Notes:

**D**

Website:
URL:
Username:
Password:
Notes:

Website:
URL:
Username:
Password:
Notes:

Website:
URL:
Username:
Password:
Notes:

Website:
URL:
Username:
Password:
Notes:

**D**

Website:
URL:
Username:
Password:
Notes:

---

Website:
URL:
Username:
Password:
Notes:

---

Website:
URL:
Username:
Password:
Notes:

---

Website:
URL:
Username:
Password:
Notes:

**D**

Website:
URL:
Username:
Password:
Notes:

Website:
URL:
Username:
Password:
Notes:

Website:
URL:
Username:
Password:
Notes:

Website:
URL:
Username:
Password:
Notes:

**D**

Website:
URL:
Username:
Password:
Notes:

Website:
URL:
Username:
Password:
Notes:

Website:
URL:
Username:
Password:
Notes:

Website:
URL:
Username:
Password:
Notes:

**E**

Website:
URL:
Username:
Password:
Notes:

Website:
URL:
Username:
Password:
Notes:

Website:
URL:
Username:
Password:
Notes:

Website:
URL:
Username:
Password:
Notes:

Website:

URL:

Username:

Password:

Notes:

---

Website:

URL:

Username:

Password:

Notes:

---

Website:

URL:

Username:

Password:

Notes:

---

Website:

URL:

Username:

Password:

Notes:

**E**

Website:
URL:
Username:
Password:
Notes:

Website:
URL:
Username:
Password:
Notes:

Website:
URL:
Username:
Password:
Notes:

Website:
URL:
Username:
Password:
Notes:

Website:
URL:
Username:
Password:
Notes:

Website:
URL:
Username:
Password:
Notes:

Website:
URL:
Username:
Password:
Notes:

Website:
URL:
Username:
Password:
Notes:

**F**

Website:
URL:
Username:
Password:
Notes:

Website:
URL:
Username:
Password:
Notes:

Website:
URL:
Username:
Password:
Notes:

Website:
URL:
Username:
Password:
Notes:

Website:
URL:
Username:
Password:
Notes:

**F**

Website:
URL:
Username:
Password:
Notes:

Website:
URL:
Username:
Password:
Notes:

Website:
URL:
Username:
Password:
Notes:

**F**

Website:
URL:
Username:
Password:
Notes:


Website:
URL:
Username:
Password:
Notes:


Website:
URL:
Username:
Password:
Notes:


Website:
URL:
Username:
Password:
Notes:

Website:

URL:

Username:

Password:

Notes:

**F**

Website:

URL:

Username:

Password:

Notes:

Website:

URL:

Username:

Password:

Notes:

Website:

URL:

Username:

Password:

Notes:

**G**

Website:

URL:

Username:

Password:

Notes:

---

Website:

URL:

Username:

Password:

Notes:

---

Website:

URL:

Username:

Password:

Notes:

---

Website:

URL:

Username:

Password:

Notes:

**G**

Website:
URL:
Username:
Password:
Notes:

Website:
URL:
Username:
Password:
Notes:

Website:
URL:
Username:
Password:
Notes:

Website:
URL:
Username:
Password:
Notes:

**G**

Website:
URL:
Username:
Password:
Notes:

Website:
URL:
Username:
Password:
Notes:

Website:
URL:
Username:
Password:
Notes:

Website:
URL:
Username:
Password:
Notes:

Website:

URL:

Username:

Password:

Notes:

G

Website:

URL:

Username:

Password:

Notes:

Website:

URL:

Username:

Password:

Notes:

Website:

URL:

Username:

Password:

Notes:

**H**

Website:
URL:
Username:
Password:
Notes:

Website:
URL:
Username:
Password:
Notes:

Website:
URL:
Username:
Password:
Notes:

Website:
URL:
Username:
Password:
Notes:

Website:

URL:

Username:

Password:

Notes:

---

Website:

URL:

Username:

Password:

Notes:

**H**

---

Website:

URL:

Username:

Password:

Notes:

---

Website:

URL:

Username:

Password:

Notes:

**H**

Website:
URL:
Username:
Password:
Notes:

Website:
URL:
Username:
Password:
Notes:

Website:
URL:
Username:
Password:
Notes:

Website:
URL:
Username:
Password:
Notes:

Website:

URL:

Username:

Password:

Notes:



**H**

Website:

URL:

Username:

Password:

Notes:



Website:

URL:

Username:

Password:

Notes:



Website:

URL:

Username:

Password:

Notes:

**I**

Website:
URL:
Username:
Password:
Notes:

---

Website:
URL:
Username:
Password:
Notes:

---

Website:
URL:
Username:
Password:
Notes:

---

Website:
URL:
Username:
Password:
Notes:

Website:
URL:
Username:
Password:
Notes:

Website:
URL:
Username:
Password:
Notes:

I

Website:
URL:
Username:
Password:
Notes:

Website:
URL:
Username:
Password:
Notes:

**I**

Website:
URL:
Username:
Password:
Notes:

Website:
URL:
Username:
Password:
Notes:

Website:
URL:
Username:
Password:
Notes:

Website:
URL:
Username:
Password:
Notes:

Website:

URL:

Username:

Password:

Notes:

Website:

URL:

Username:

Password:

Notes:

I

Website:

URL:

Username:

Password:

Notes:

Website:

URL:

Username:

Password:

Notes:

**J**

Website:
URL:
Username:
Password:
Notes:


Website:
URL:
Username:
Password:
Notes:


Website:
URL:
Username:
Password:
Notes:


Website:
URL:
Username:
Password:
Notes:

Website:

URL:

Username:

Password:

Notes:


Website:

URL:

Username:

Password:

Notes:

J


Website:

URL:

Username:

Password:

Notes:


Website:

URL:

Username:

Password:

Notes:

**J**

Website:
URL:
Username:
Password:
Notes:

Website:
URL:
Username:
Password:
Notes:

Website:
URL:
Username:
Password:
Notes:

Website:
URL:
Username:
Password:
Notes:

Website:

URL:

Username:

Password:

Notes:


Website:

URL:

Username:

Password:

Notes:

J

Website:

URL:

Username:

Password:

Notes:


Website:

URL:

Username:

Password:

Notes:

**K**

Website:
URL:
Username:
Password:
Notes:

Website:
URL:
Username:
Password:
Notes:

Website:
URL:
Username:
Password:
Notes:

Website:
URL:
Username:
Password:
Notes:

Website:

URL:

Username:

Password:

Notes:



Website:

URL:

Username:

Password:

Notes:

Website:

URL:

Username:

Password:

Notes:



Website:

URL:

Username:

Password:

Notes:

**K**

Website:
URL:
Username:
Password:
Notes:

Website:
URL:
Username:
Password:
Notes:

Website:
URL:
Username:
Password:
Notes:

Website:
URL:
Username:
Password:
Notes:

Website:

URL:

Username:

Password:

Notes:

---

Website:

URL:

Username:

Password:

Notes:

---

Website:

URL:

Username:

Password:

Notes:

---

Website:

URL:

Username:

Password:

Notes:

**L**

Website:

URL:

Username:

Password:

Notes:

---

Website:

URL:

Username:

Password:

Notes:

---

Website:

URL:

Username:

Password:

Notes:

---

Website:

URL:

Username:

Password:

Notes:

Website:

URL:

Username:

Password:

Notes:

---

Website:

URL:

Username:

Password:

Notes:

**L**

---

Website:

URL:

Username:

Password:

Notes:

---

Website:

URL:

Username:

Password:

Notes:

**L**

Website:
URL:
Username:
Password:
Notes:

Website:
URL:
Username:
Password:
Notes:

Website:
URL:
Username:
Password:
Notes:

Website:
URL:
Username:
Password:
Notes:

Website:
URL:
Username:
Password:
Notes:

Website:
URL:
Username:
Password:
Notes:

L

Website:
URL:
Username:
Password:
Notes:

Website:
URL:
Username:
Password:
Notes:

**M**

Website:
URL:
Username:
Password:
Notes:

Website:
URL:
Username:
Password:
Notes:

Website:
URL:
Username:
Password:
Notes:

Website:
URL:
Username:
Password:
Notes:

Website:

URL:

Username:

Password:

Notes:



Website:

URL:

Username:

Password:

Notes:

M

Website:

URL:

Username:

Password:

Notes:



Website:

URL:

Username:

Password:

Notes:

**M**

Website:
URL:
Username:
Password:
Notes:

Website:
URL:
Username:
Password:
Notes:

Website:
URL:
Username:
Password:
Notes:

Website:
URL:
Username:
Password:
Notes:

Website:

URL:

Username:

Password:

Notes:

Website:

URL:

Username:

Password:

Notes:

M

Website:

URL:

Username:

Password:

Notes:

Website:

URL:

Username:

Password:

Notes:

**N**

Website:
URL:
Username:
Password:
Notes:

Website:
URL:
Username:
Password:
Notes:

Website:
URL:
Username:
Password:
Notes:

Website:
URL:
Username:
Password:
Notes:

Website:

URL:

Username:

Password:

Notes:

---

Website:

URL:

Username:

Password:

Notes:

---

N

Website:

URL:

Username:

Password:

Notes:

---

Website:

URL:

Username:

Password:

Notes:

Website:

URL:

Username:

Password:

Notes:



Website:

URL:

Username:

Password:

Notes:



**N**

Website:

URL:

Username:

Password:

Notes:



Website:

URL:

Username:

Password:

Notes:

| Website: | |
| --- | --- |
| URL: | |
| Username: | |
| Password: | |
| Notes: | |

| Website: | |
| --- | --- |
| URL: | |
| Username: | |
| Password: | |
| Notes: | |

**N**

| Website: | |
| --- | --- |
| URL: | |
| Username: | |
| Password: | |
| Notes: | |

| Website: | |
| --- | --- |
| URL: | |
| Username: | |
| Password: | |
| Notes: | |

**O**

Website:
URL:
Username:
Password:
Notes:


Website:
URL:
Username:
Password:
Notes:


Website:
URL:
Username:
Password:
Notes:


Website:
URL:
Username:
Password:
Notes:

Website:

URL:

Username:

Password:

Notes:

---

Website:

URL:

Username:

Password:

Notes:

---

Website:

URL:

Username:

Password:

Notes:

O

---

Website:

URL:

Username:

Password:

Notes:

**O**

Website:
URL:
Username:
Password:
Notes:


Website:
URL:
Username:
Password:
Notes:


Website:
URL:
Username:
Password:
Notes:


Website:
URL:
Username:
Password:
Notes:

Website:

URL:

Username:

Password:

Notes:

---

Website:

URL:

Username:

Password:

Notes:

---

Website:

URL:

O

Username:

Password:

Notes:

---

Website:

URL:

Username:

Password:

Notes:

**P**

Website:
URL:
Username:
Password:
Notes:

Website:
URL:
Username:
Password:
Notes:

Website:
URL:
Username:
Password:
Notes:

Website:
URL:
Username:
Password:
Notes:

**Website:**

**URL:**

**Username:**

**Password:**

**Notes:**


**Website:**

**URL:**

**Username:**

**Password:**

**Notes:**


**Website:**

**URL:**

**Username:**

**Password:**

**Notes:**

P

**Website:**

**URL:**

**Username:**

**Password:**

**Notes:**

**P**

Website:
URL:
Username:
Password:
Notes:

Website:
URL:
Username:
Password:
Notes:

Website:
URL:
Username:
Password:
Notes:

Website:
URL:
Username:
Password:
Notes:

Website:

URL:

Username:

Password:

Notes:

---

Website:

URL:

Username:

Password:

Notes:

---

Website:

URL:

Username:

Password:

Notes:

**P**

---

Website:

URL:

Username:

Password:

Notes:

Website:

URL:

Username:

Password:

Notes:

---

Website:

URL:

Username:

Password:

Notes:

---

**Q**

Website:

URL:

Username:

Password:

Notes:

---

Website:

URL:

Username:

Password:

Notes:

Website:

URL:

Username:

Password:

Notes:

---

Website:

URL:

Username:

Password:

Notes:

---

Website:

URL:

Username:

Password:

Notes:

Q

---

Website:

URL:

Username:

Password:

Notes:

**Q**

Website: _____
URL: _____
Username: _____
Password: _____
Notes: _____
_____
_____
_____

Website: _____
URL: _____
Username: _____
Password: _____
Notes: _____
_____
_____
_____

Website: _____
URL: _____
Username: _____
Password: _____
Notes: _____
_____
_____
_____

Website: _____
URL: _____
Username: _____
Password: _____
Notes: _____
_____
_____
_____

**Website:**

**URL:**

**Username:**

**Password:**

**Notes:**


---

**Website:**

**URL:**

**Username:**

**Password:**

**Notes:**


---

**Website:**

**URL:**

**Username:**

**Password:**

**Notes:**

Q


---

**Website:**

**URL:**

**Username:**

**Password:**

**Notes:**

**Website:**

**URL:**

**Username:**

**Password:**

**Notes:**

---

**Website:**

**URL:**

**Username:**

**Password:**

**Notes:**

---

R

**Website:**

**URL:**

**Username:**

**Password:**

**Notes:**

---

**Website:**

**URL:**

**Username:**

**Password:**

**Notes:**

Website:

URL:

Username:

Password:

Notes:


Website:

URL:

Username:

Password:

Notes:


Website:

URL:

Username:

Password:

Notes:

R


Website:

URL:

Username:

Password:

Notes:

Website:

URL:

Username:

Password:

Notes:


Website:

URL:

Username:

Password:

Notes:


**R**

Website:

URL:

Username:

Password:

Notes:


Website:

URL:

Username:

Password:

Notes:

Website:

URL:

Username:

Password:

Notes:




Website:

URL:

Username:

Password:

Notes:




Website:

URL:

Username:

Password:

Notes:

R




Website:

URL:

Username:

Password:

Notes:

Website:

URL:

Username:

Password:

Notes:




Website:

URL:

Username:

Password:

Notes:




Website:

URL:

Username:

Password:

Notes:

S



Website:

URL:

Username:

Password:

Notes:

Website:

URL:

Username:

Password:

Notes:

---

Website:

URL:

Username:

Password:

Notes:

---

Website:

URL:

Username:

Password:

Notes:

S

Website:

URL:

Username:

Password:

Notes:

Website:

URL:

Username:

Password:

Notes:

---

Website:

URL:

Username:

Password:

Notes:

---

Website:

URL:

Username:

Password:

Notes:

**S**

---

Website:

URL:

Username:

Password:

Notes:

Website:

URL:

Username:

Password:

Notes:

---

Website:

URL:

Username:

Password:

Notes:

---

Website:

URL:

Username:

Password:

Notes:

S

---

Website:

URL:

Username:

Password:

Notes:

Website:

URL:

Username:

Password:

Notes:




Website:

URL:

Username:

Password:

Notes:




Website:

URL:

Username:

Password:

Notes:



T

Website:

URL:

Username:

Password:

Notes:

Website:

URL:

Username:

Password:

Notes:


Website:

URL:

Username:

Password:

Notes:


Website:

URL:

Username:

Password:

Notes:

T

Website:

URL:

Username:

Password:

Notes:

**T**

Website:
URL:
Username:
Password:
Notes:


Website:
URL:
Username:
Password:
Notes:


Website:
URL:
Username:
Password:
Notes:


Website:
URL:
Username:
Password:
Notes:

Website:

URL:

Username:

Password:

Notes:

---

Website:

URL:

Username:

Password:

Notes:

---

Website:

URL:

Username:

Password:

Notes:

---

T

Website:

URL:

Username:

Password:

Notes:

**U**

Website:
URL:
Username:
Password:
Notes:

Website:
URL:
Username:
Password:
Notes:

Website:
URL:
Username:
Password:
Notes:

Website:
URL:
Username:
Password:
Notes:

Website:

URL:

Username:

Password:

Notes:

Website:

URL:

Username:

Password:

Notes:

Website:

URL:

Username:

Password:

Notes:

Website:

URL:

Username:

Password:

Notes:

U

Website:
URL:
Username:
Password:
Notes:


Website:
URL:
Username:
Password:
Notes:


Website:
URL:
Username:
Password:
Notes:


**U**

Website:
URL:
Username:
Password:
Notes:

Website:

URL:

Username:

Password:

Notes:



Website:

URL:

Username:

Password:

Notes:



Website:

URL:

Username:

Password:

Notes:



Website:

URL:

Username:

Password:

Notes:

U

Website:

URL:

Username:

Password:

Notes:

---

Website:

URL:

Username:

Password:

Notes:

---

Website:

URL:

Username:

Password:

Notes:

---

**V**

Website:

URL:

Username:

Password:

Notes:

Website:

URL:

Username:

Password:

Notes:

---

Website:

URL:

Username:

Password:

Notes:

---

Website:

URL:

Username:

Password:

Notes:

---

Website:

URL:

V

Username:

Password:

Notes:

Website:
URL:
Username:
Password:
Notes:

---

Website:
URL:
Username:
Password:
Notes:

---

Website:
URL:
Username:
Password:
Notes:

---

**V**

Website:
URL:
Username:
Password:
Notes:

Website:
URL:
Username:
Password:
Notes:

Website:
URL:
Username:
Password:
Notes:

Website:
URL:
Username:
Password:
Notes:

Website:
URL:
Username:
Password:
Notes:

V

Website:
URL:
Username:
Password:
Notes:

Website:
URL:
Username:
Password:
Notes:

Website:
URL:
Username:
Password:
Notes:

**W**

Website:
URL:
Username:
Password:
Notes:

**Website:**

**URL:**

**Username:**

**Password:**

**Notes:**

---

**Website:**

**URL:**

**Username:**

**Password:**

**Notes:**

---

**Website:**

**URL:**

**Username:**

**Password:**

**Notes:**

---

**Website:**

**URL:**

**Username:**

**Password:**

**Notes:**

W

**Website:**

**URL:**

**Username:**

**Password:**

**Notes:**

---

**Website:**

**URL:**

**Username:**

**Password:**

**Notes:**

---

**Website:**

**URL:**

**Username:**

**Password:**

**Notes:**

---

W

**Website:**

**URL:**

**Username:**

**Password:**

**Notes:**

| | |
|---|---|
| Website: | |
| URL: | |
| Username: | |
| Password: | |
| Notes: | |
| | |
| | |

| | |
|---|---|
| Website: | |
| URL: | |
| Username: | |
| Password: | |
| Notes: | |
| | |
| | |

| | |
|---|---|
| Website: | |
| URL: | |
| Username: | |
| Password: | |
| Notes: | |
| | |
| | |

| | |
|---|---|
| Website: | |
| URL: | |
| Username: | |
| Password: | |
| Notes: | |
| | |
| | |

W

Website:

URL:

Username:

Password:

Notes:

---

Website:

URL:

Username:

Password:

Notes:

---

Website:

URL:

Username:

Password:

Notes:

---

Website:

URL:

Username:

Password:

X

Notes:

Website:

URL:

Username:

Password:

Notes:




Website:

URL:

Username:

Password:

Notes:




Website:

URL:

Username:

Password:

Notes:




Website:

URL:

Username:

Password:

Notes:

X

Website: _____

URL: _____

Username: _____

Password: _____

Notes: _____

_____

_____

Website: _____

URL: _____

Username: _____

Password: _____

Notes: _____

_____

_____

Website: _____

URL: _____

Username: _____

Password: _____

Notes: _____

_____

_____

**X**

Website: _____

URL: _____

Username: _____

Password: _____

Notes: _____

_____

_____

Website:
URL:
Username:
Password:
Notes:



Website:
URL:
Username:
Password:
Notes:



Website:
URL:
Username:
Password:
Notes:



Website:
URL:
Username:
Password:
Notes:

X

Website:
URL:
Username:
Password:
Notes:

Website:
URL:
Username:
Password:
Notes:

Website:
URL:
Username:
Password:
Notes:

Website:
URL:
Username:
Password:
Notes:

Y

Website:

URL:

Username:

Password:

Notes:

---

Website:

URL:

Username:

Password:

Notes:

---

Website:

URL:

Username:

Password:

Notes:

---

Website:

URL:

Username:

Password:

Notes:

Y

Website:

URL:

Username:

Password:

Notes:

Website:

URL:

Username:

Password:

Notes:

Website:

URL:

Username:

Password:

Notes:

Website:

URL:

Username:

Password:

Notes:

Y

Website:

URL:

Username:

Password:

Notes:



Website:

URL:

Username:

Password:

Notes:



Website:

URL:

Username:

Password:

Notes:



Website:

URL:

Username:

Password:

Notes:

Website:

URL:

Username:

Password:

Notes:

---

Website:

URL:

Username:

Password:

Notes:

---

Website:

URL:

Username:

Password:

Notes:

---

Website:

URL:

Username:

Password:

Notes:

Z

Website:

URL:

Username:

Password:

Notes:

---

Website:

URL:

Username:

Password:

Notes:

---

Website:

URL:

Username:

Password:

Notes:

---

Website:

URL:

Username:

Password:

Notes:

Z

**Website:**

**URL:**

**Username:**

**Password:**

**Notes:**

---

**Website:**

**URL:**

**Username:**

**Password:**

**Notes:**

---

**Website:**

**URL:**

**Username:**

**Password:**

**Notes:**

---

**Website:**

**URL:**

**Username:**

**Password:**

**Notes:**

Z

Website:

URL:

Username:

Password:

Notes:




Website:

URL:

Username:

Password:

Notes:




Website:

URL:

Username:

Password:

Notes:




Website:

URL:

Username:

Password:

Notes:



Z

Website:

URL:

Username:

Password:

Notes:



Website:

URL:

Username:

Password:

Notes:



Website:

URL:

Username:

Password:

Notes:



Website:

URL:

Username:

Password:

Notes:

Website:

URL:

Username:

Password:

Notes:




Website:

URL:

Username:

Password:

Notes:




Website:

URL:

Username:

Password:

Notes:




Website:

URL:

Username:

Password:

Notes:

Website:

URL:

Username:

Password:

Notes:


Website:

URL:

Username:

Password:

Notes:


Website:

URL:

Username:

Password:

Notes:


Website:

URL:

Username:

Password:

Notes:

Website: _____

URL: _____

Username: _____

Password: _____

Notes: _____

_____

_____

_____

Website: _____

URL: _____

Username: _____

Password: _____

Notes: _____

_____

_____

_____

Website: _____

URL: _____

Username: _____

Password: _____

Notes: _____

_____

_____

_____

Website: _____

URL: _____

Username: _____

Password: _____

Notes: _____

_____

_____